D1199034

J793.8
Oakley, Ruth
Games with Papers and Pencils

DISCARD

FORBUSH MEMORIAL LIBRARY

MAIN STREET

WESTMINSTER, MA. 01473

Games with Papers and Pencils

THE MARSHALL CAVENDISH ILLUSTRATED GUIDE TO

GAMES CHILDREN PLAY AROUND THE WORLD

Games with Papers and Pencils

Ruth Oakley

Illustrated by Steve Lucas

WESTMINSTER LIBRARY   DISCARD

Marshall Cavendish
New York · London · Toronto · Sydney

Library Edition 1989

© Marshall Cavendish Limited 1989
© DPM Services Limited 1989

Published by Marshall Cavendish Corporation
           147 West Merrick Road
           Freeport
           Long Island
           N.Y. 11520

Produced by DPM Services Limited
Designed by Graham Beehag

All rights reserved. No part of this book may be reproduced or
utilized in any form or by any means electronic or mechanical
including photocopying, recording, or by an information storage and
retrieval system, without permission from the copyright holders.

Library of Congress Cataloging-in-Publication Data

Oakley, Ruth.
    Games with papers and pencils/written by Ruth Oakley:
Illustrated by Steve Lucas.
    p.   cm—(Games children play)
    Includes index.
    Summary: Gives instructions for a selection of games using paper
and pencil.
    ISBN 1-85435-083-8
    1. Pencil games—Juvenile literature. [1. Pencil games.
2. Games.] I. Lucas, Steve, [1]. II. Title. III. Series: Oakley,
Ruth. Games children play.
GV1493.02 1989
793.8—dc19   88-28711
                                           CIP
                                           AC

ISBN 1-85435-076-5 (set)

Printed and bound in Italy by L.E.G.O. SpA, Vicenza

Contents

It was the Chinese who first discovered how to make paper about two thousand years ago. Before that, the Egyptians, Greeks, and Romans had used papyrus, which was a water reed. The Romans also used parchment made from animal skins.

Probably the best known toy made from paper is a **kite**. In Eastern countries such as China, Japan, Malaysia, and Korea, the arts of kite-making and kite-flying are taken more seriously than in Western countries and have many traditions associated with them.

This old woodcut shows children flying kites with tails made of pieces of cloth.

The Chinese make very elaborate kites.

In some areas, flying kites over a house at night was believed to keep away evil spirits. Some people in Korea and Malaysia write the year's misfortunes on a kite in the hope that their troubles will fly away when they fly the kite.

Sometimes, kite fights are held in Oriental countries. The kite strings are covered in glue and sharp fragments of glass or earthenware are brushed on. If the kites are flown so that their strings cross, one of the strings will be cut, and the kite will fall to the ground.

A Greek, Archytas of Tarentum, made kites in the fifth century B.C. In 1752, Benjamin Franklin demonstrated the electrical nature of lightning by flying a kite with a metal key attached to it during a storm. At the beginning of the twentieth century, Marconi used a kite in his experiment to send the first wireless radio communication across the Atlantic.

Kites have also been used for weather observation.

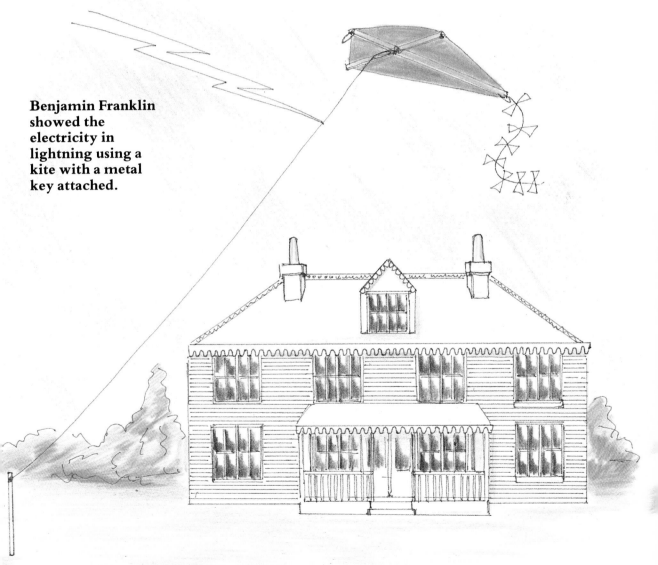

Benjamin Franklin showed the electricity in lightning using a kite with a metal key attached.

The English word "kite" comes from the fact that the shape of kites usually flown in England looks like the shape of a bird of prey called a kite. In France, a kite is called "cerf-volant," which means "flying stag." The Japanese call kites "tako," which means "octopus." In India, the word is "patang," which means "feather."

The materials for making a kite must be light and strong, and very successful kites can be made from paper. There are many different designs for making kites, including the box type, first made by an Australian named Lawrence Hargrave in the 1890s. Of course, you can buy kites very easily. Plastic ones can be inexpensive, and there are special, more expensive kites for stunt flying.

It is quite easy — and much more satisfying — to make your own kite. Directions are given here for one type. If you want to be more adventurous, there are lots of other books available to give you ideas.

To make a simple kite which is easy to fly, you will need:

* 2 straight, light, strong sticks (strips of balsa wood or very thin doweling work well): one 24in. long; one 18in. long.
* 1 piece of strong, thin paper about 30 in. square for the kite and 50 pieces of tissue paper 8in. square to make the tail.
* 2yds. of wide cotton tape or thick string.
* 1 metal ring (a curtain ring or a key ring would do).
* string or thin wire.
* tape or glue.
* poster paints or felt-tip pens to decorate your kite.
* spool and 100yds. of thin, strong cotton string for flying the kite.

Drill a small hole at each end of the two sticks (four holes). (You may need help with this.)

Fasten the two sticks together with the string or wire to make a cross (see diagram.) Make sure the arms of the cross are equal so that the kite will be balanced. Tie a loop of string where the arms cross so that you can attach the bridle when you are ready to fly your kite.

Thread a piece of string about 3ft. long through the four holes, starting at the top. Tie the string firmly at the top and make two more loops, one at the top and one at the bottom. The string should be taut without making the sticks bend.

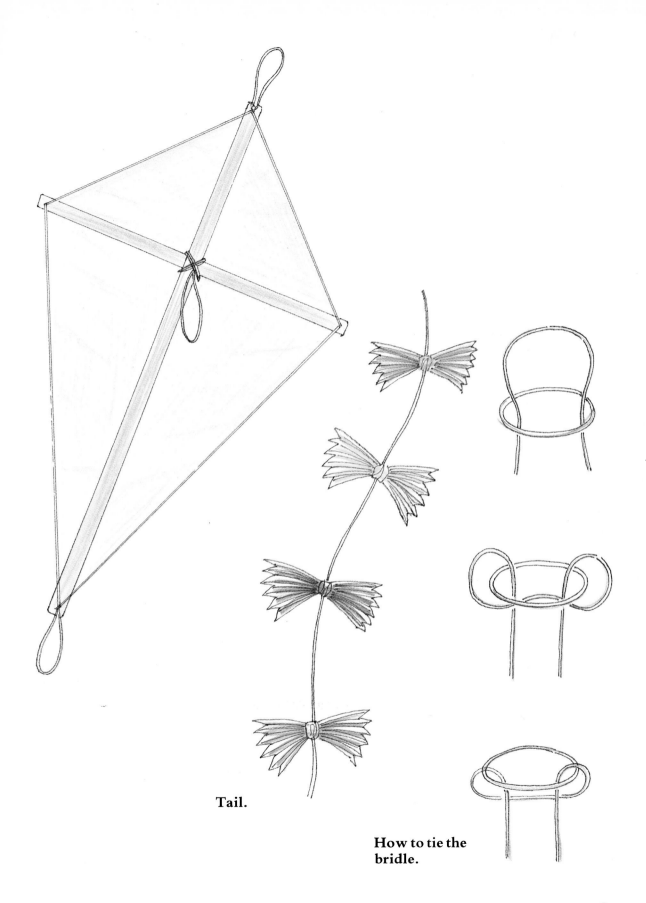

Tail.

How to tie the bridle.

SAFETY

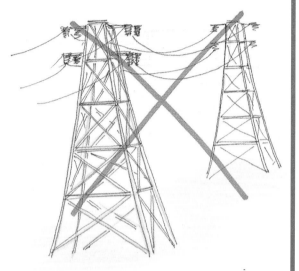

NEVER FLY A KITE IN
WET WEATHER—
REMEMBER BENJAMIN
FRANKLIN'S
EXPERIMENT!

FLY IN AN OPEN
SPACE, WELL AWAY
FROM OVERHEAD
CABLES, TREES,
AND BUILDINGS.

IF YOUR KITE GETS
TANGLED IN A
HIGH TREE OR
OVERHEAD WIRES,
LEAVE IT!

Place the "cross" flat on the paper, and cut out a "kite" shape to fit the string, leaving a margin of about an inch so that you can fold the paper over the string and fasten it down with tape or glue. Make the paper as tight and smooth as possible.

Cut a small hole in the paper and pull the center loop through.

Decorate your kite.

Make the tail by folding up the pieces of tissue paper, tying them in the middle at intervals of 6in. along a piece of string 15 yds. long.

Tie the tail to the bottom loop.

Make the bridle by cutting the tape into two pieces. The first should be about half a yard long, leaving about one and a half yards for the other. Fasten the short piece securely to the ring and to the loop you made at the top of your kite. Use the special knot shown in the diagrams to fasten the long piece to the ring and then attach one end to the loop at the middle of the cross and the other end to the string on your spool.

The knot on the ring allows you to adjust the bridle easily according to the weather conditions. The windier the weather, the nearer to the kite the ring will need to be.

You are now ready to go out and fly your kite.

The weather does not need to be very windy: a gentle breeze is ideal.

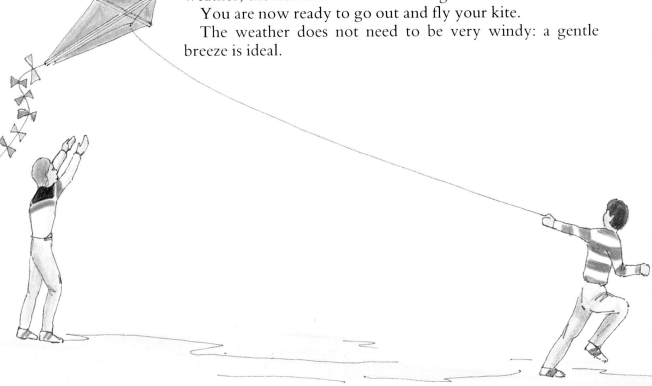

Origami is a Japanese word, "ori" means "folding," and "gami" means "paper." Origami, or paper-folding, is a very old art and one which people of all ages in many countries enjoy. It is possible to produce very complicated models with as many as two hundred folds. There are also plenty of interesting things you can make which are very simple.

This book will explain how to make three toys just by folding paper. If you want to learn more about origami, there are many books about it; in some places, there are also clubs, societies, and classes where you can learn more.

To make a boat which will really float, you need a piece of plain typing paper.

1. Fold it in half lengthwise. Be careful to make sure the corners meet and that you make a straight, sharp crease.
2. Unfold the paper and make a fold widthwise.
3. Place the paper so that the fold is at the top. Then fold over the two top corners so that they meet in the middle of the paper along the original lengthwise fold line.
4. There is now a section of the paper at the bottom which is still only double thickness. Fold the top layer up to meet the two triangles which you made in step 3.
5. Fold the corners of the piece you just folded behind the two large triangles.
6. Fold the remaining bottom flap behind the two large triangles.
7. Hold the paper by the original lengthwise fold, and pull it out to make a square standing on one of its corners.
8. Hold the bottom corners. Fold the top layer up to about 2/3 of the diagonal crease, and fold the bottom layer underneath to match.
9. Open out the paper on the other folds again as you did in step 7.
10. Hold the tops of the two small triangles and pull gently. Press flat and then open the base slightly. Your boat is now ready to be named and launched!

If you make several as a group project, you can have races.

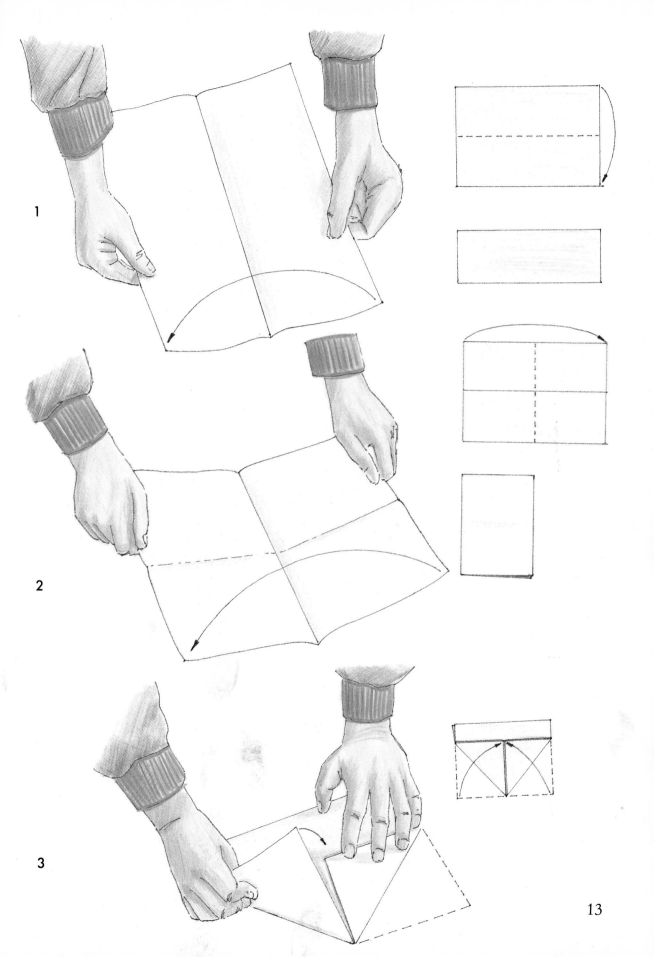

1

2

3

13

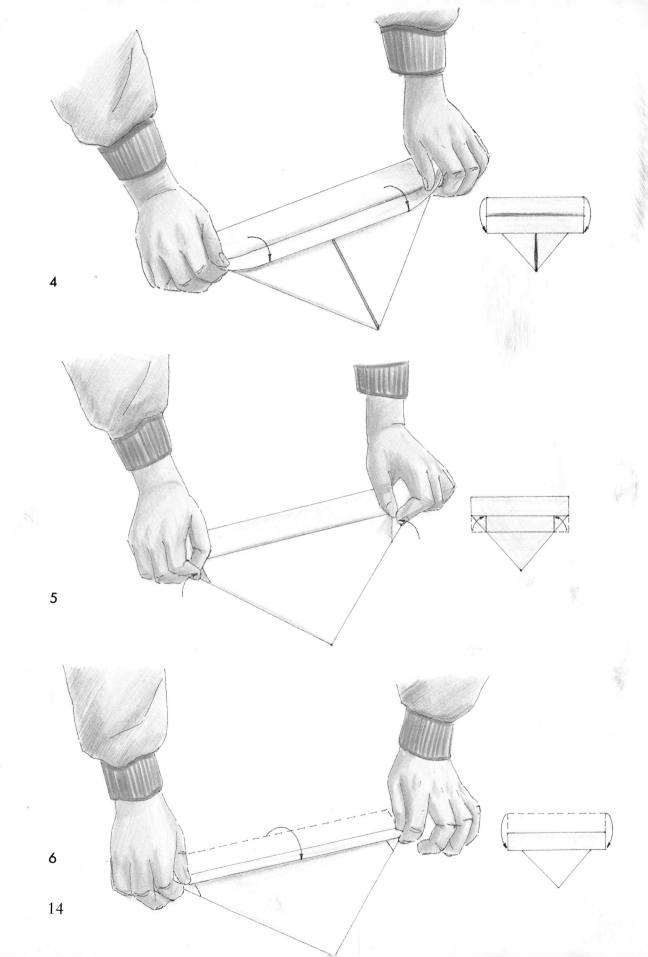

4

5

6

14

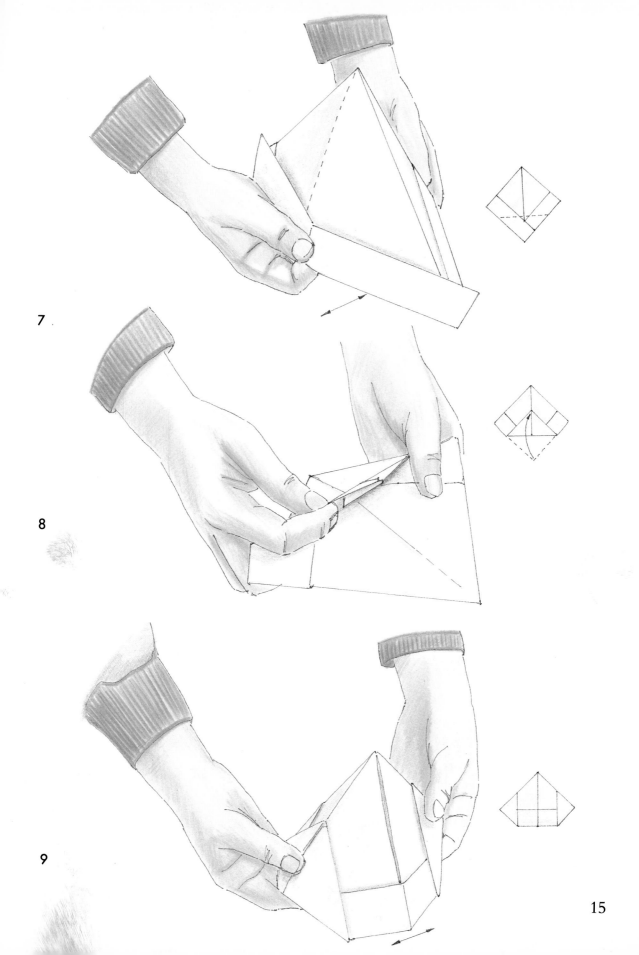

7

8

9

10

11

Whole books have been written on how to make **paper airplanes**. Directions are given here for a very simple design which flies successfully.

1. Fold a piece of plain typing paper lengthwise.
2. Place the paper with the fold at the top and fold the bottom lefthand corners to meet the top fold. The top layer is folded forward, and the bottom layer is folded to the back.
3. Repeat step 2. Be careful to make your folds accurately so that the top and bottom folds are the same. Otherwise, your plane will have uneven wings and will not fly properly.
4. Fold the sloping edges up to meet the top fold.

Your airplane is ready to fly. Hold it between finger and thumb under the wings and throw it gently forward and up. If you make several with a group of friends, you can have contests to see which plane will fly farthest.

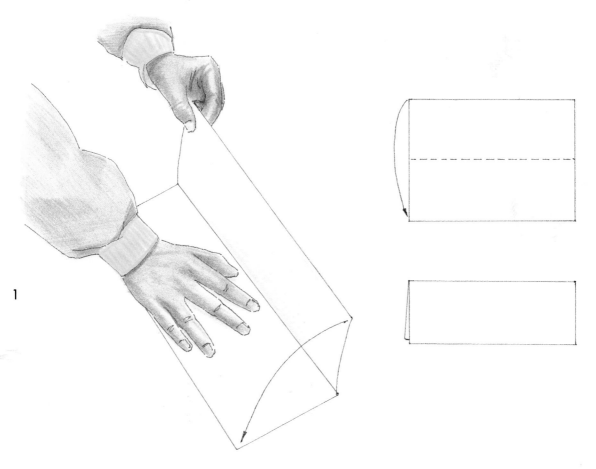

1

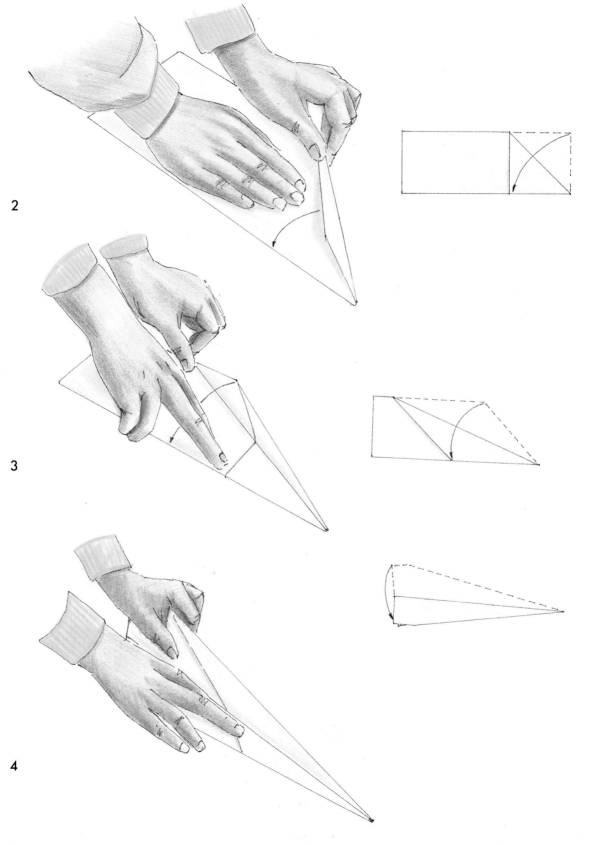

2

3

4

5

6

Make a **Fortune Teller** using a piece of plain 8x10 typing paper which is neither very thick nor very thin.

1. Fold the bottom edge across to meet a side edge. Since the paper is not square, there will be a single thickness of paper at the top, which must be trimmed away carefully to make a square piece of paper.
2. Open the square and make another diagonal fold in the opposite direction.
3. Open the square again and fold each corner in turn to touch the center where the two diagonal folds intersect.
4. Turn over the folded paper so that the folds are underneath it, and fold the new set of corners to the middle point in the same way as you did in step 3.
5. Turn the paper over so that you see four squares divided by a cross.
6. Fold the paper in half horizontally and then vertically; then open it out again as it was.
7. Hold the paper with the four squares underneath. Place the index finger and thumb of each hand into each one of the squares. Push your fingers and thumbs up into the points; you should find that the folded paper has a kind of double "mouth" which you can open and close by moving your fingers.

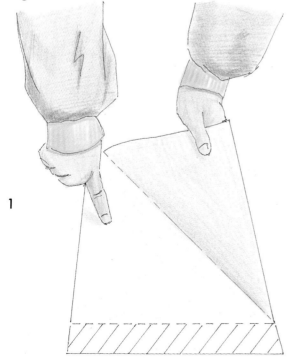

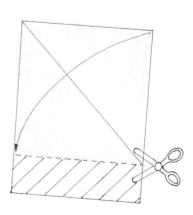

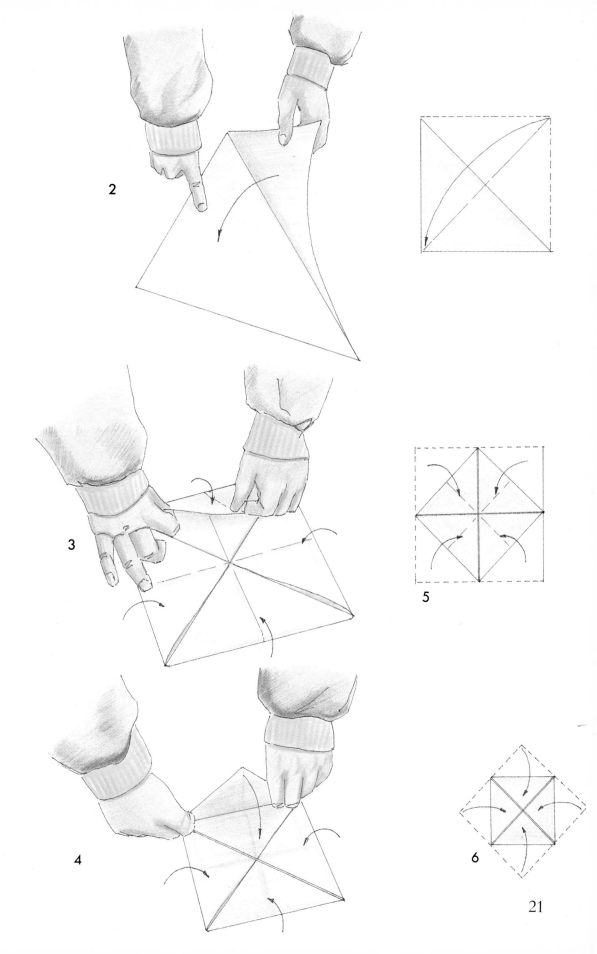

2

3

4

5

6

21

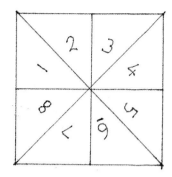

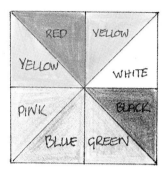

7

Now, fold the Fortune Teller flat again and begin coloring and labeling it so that you can use it to play with your friends.

First, label or color each half of the four squares with a different color: you will need to use eight different colors.

Turn the paper over, and number each of the eight triangles on the other side from "1" to "8." Then, open up the four triangular flaps and write eight different "fortune-telling" messages on the backs of the flaps. Fold the Fortune Teller back as it was. Now you are ready to tell someone's fortune.

First, ask her to choose one of your eight colors. Spell the color aloud, opening and closing the Fortune Teller on each letter. Then, she chooses one of the four numbers which are visible. Open and close the Fortune Teller that number of times. She chooses again from the numbers she can see this time. Open the flap which has that number on it, and read out what is written underneath it to tell her fortune.

The more amusing you can make your messages, the better people will like it. They will find it quite difficult to get the message they would like, even if they hear other people's turns.

Tangram is a game which originally came from China, but it is now played around the world. You can buy a set of pieces, but it is very easy to make your own. You will need a piece of thick paper or thin cardboard 5in. square, a sharp pencil, a ruler, and a pair of scissors.

1. Draw a diagonal line from the bottom lefthand corner to the top righthand corner of the square, using a ruler.
2. Measure and mark halfway along the bottom line and halfway up the righthand side. Join these marks with a straight line.
3. Draw another diagonal line from the top lefthand corner, but stop when you reach the line you drew in Step 2.
4. From the point where the lines which you drew in Steps 2 and 3 intersect, draw a vertical line to meet the diagonal line which you drew in Step 1.
5. Measure 1¼in. from the bottom corner of the square, and lightly draw a vertical dotted line up to meet the diagonal you drew in Step 1. Make a mark where they intersect.
6. Using the ruler, draw a line from the mark made in Step 5

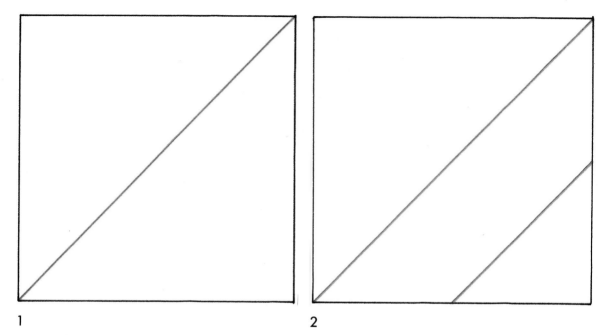

1

2

to the mark halfway along the bottom which you made in Step 2.

7. Cut out the pieces carefully. You should have five triangles, a square, and a parallelogram.

Now see how many different silhouettes of everyday objects you can make. More than two thousand designs have been published. To play Tangram as a game with your friends, see who can make a particular shape first. Each player must use every piece. The pieces must not overlap, but you are allowed to have gaps between the pieces.

Try to make geometric shapes like a rectangle or a triangle, or imaginative ones like the cat shown in the drawing.

Or, experiment with the way you cut up the original square. An easier game is for everyone to have a piece of paper 3in. square and a pair of scissors. Each player cuts his square twice to make four different-shaped pieces. Mix up the four pieces and pass them to the next player to be reassembled.

Another game from China is **Double Sixes**. It is a game for two players, or for four playing as partners.

The equipment you need is thirty-two counters in two colors (sixteen of each color), a large piece of thick paper, thirty small pieces of paper, and a container such as a bowl or basket to put the pieces of paper in.

You can either make your own counters from cardboard,

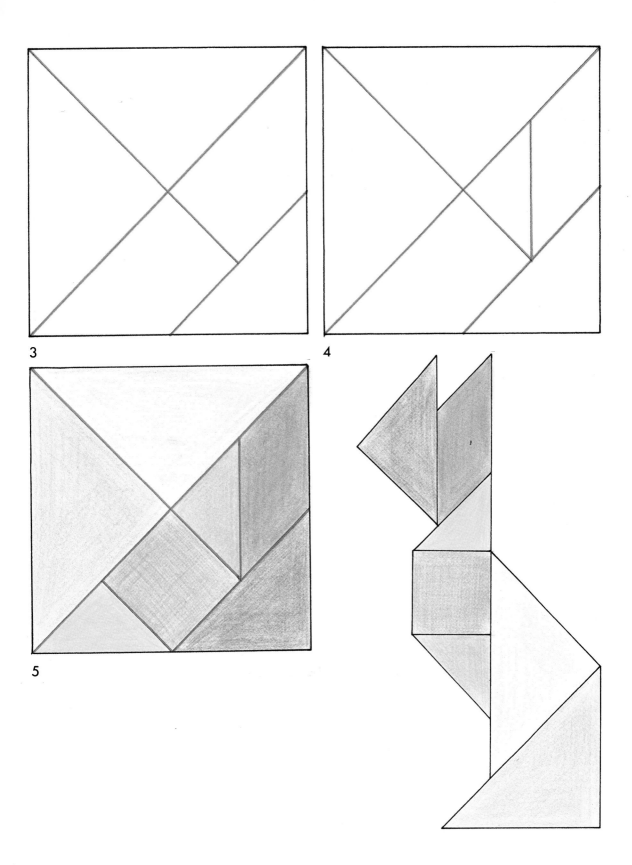

3

4

5

or use some from another game, or use buttons or bottle tops.

Using a ruler or yardstick, divide the large piece of paper into squares by drawing 8 horizontal lines and 28 vertical ones. The players sit at the narrow ends of the paper, and the two rows of squares nearest to them make up their fields (sixteen squares each).

Write the following messages on the small pieces of paper. "Place horse in field" (make 4). "Turn right" (make 2). "Turn left" (make 2). "Ride forward" (make 6). "Jump the horse in front" (make 4). "Gallop 6 squares" (make 2). "Move backward" (make 2). "Back to the left" (make 2). "Back to the right" (make 2). "Stand still" (make 2). "Move a horse to your opponent's field" (make 2).

To begin the game, each player puts eight "horses" (counters) on the first row of eight squares on his or her field. The direction slips are mixed up in the bowl, and each player takes turns in drawing a slip and following its instruction. Each slip is returned to the bowl each time, and the papers are mixed up after each turn.

If an opponent's horse is on the square which you move to, it must be removed, and your opponent will have to wait for a "Place horse in field" slip.

The aim of the game is to be the first to get all sixteen of your horses onto your opponent's field.

To play **Beetle, Bug,** or **Cootie,** you need one ordinary die and a piece of paper and a pencil for each player. Any number of children of any age can play.

The object of the game is to be the first to draw a complete beetle, but you can only draw each part according to the number you throw on the die. Each player has one throw of the die and then passes it to the player on the right. You cannot start until you have thrown a "1" on your turn, which allows you to draw the beetle's body. After you have drawn the body, you add the head, the legs, and the tail. You need a "2" for the head. You add one leg each time you throw a "3" and a tail if you throw a "6."

You may not draw eyes and feelers until you have first drawn the head. You need a "4" for each eye and a "5" for each feeler.

The winning beetle has to have six legs, two eyes, two feelers, and one body, one head, and one tail. When your beetle is complete, the winner shouts, "Beetle."

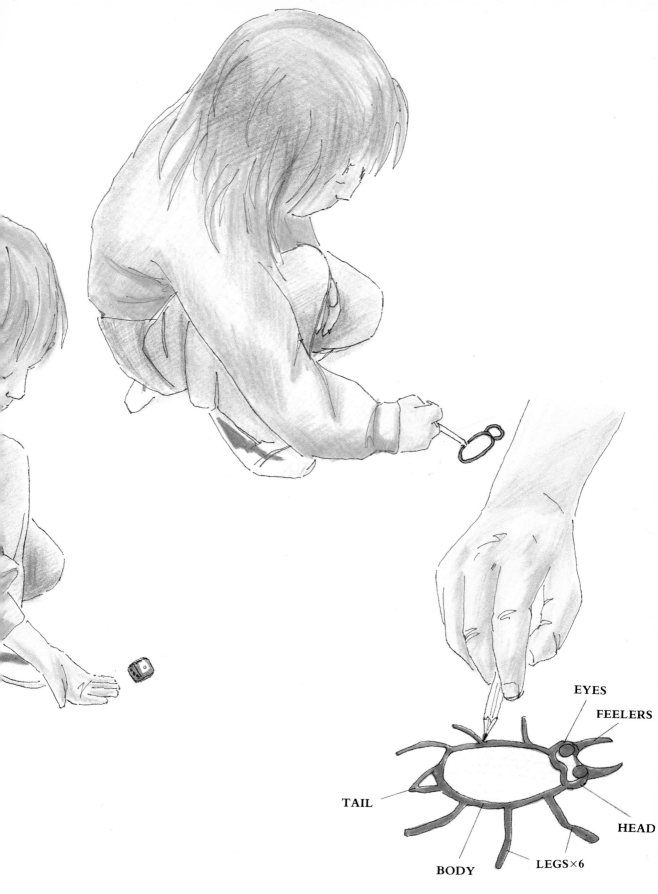

EYES

FEELERS

TAIL

HEAD

BODY

LEGS×6

If you do not have a die, you can make a teetotum or spinner out of thick paper or cardboard. You need compasses, a pencil, and a pair of scissors.

With the compasses, draw a circle with a radius of 1¼in. Keep the compasses set at 1¼in., place the point of the compasses anywhere on the circumference of the circle and make a mark on the circle with the pencil.

Move the point of the compasses to the mark and make another mark. Repeat until you have made six marks — you should be back where you started.

Using a ruler, draw six lines from the center of the circle to the six marks on the circumference, and draw lines from each point on the circumference to the next. This will make a regular hexagon (a six-sided shape with equal sides).

Cut out the hexagon carefully and push a toothpick through the center. Then either draw the parts of the beetle — body, head, eye, leg, feeler, and tail — or write the numbers "1" to "6."

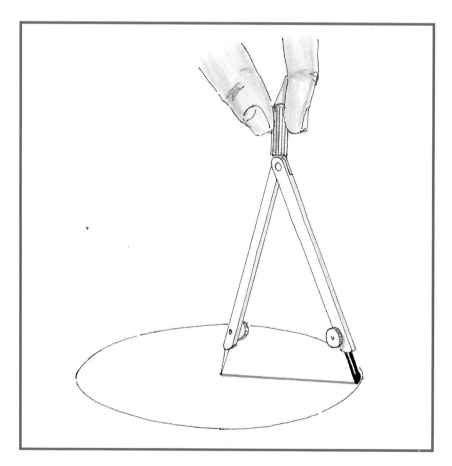

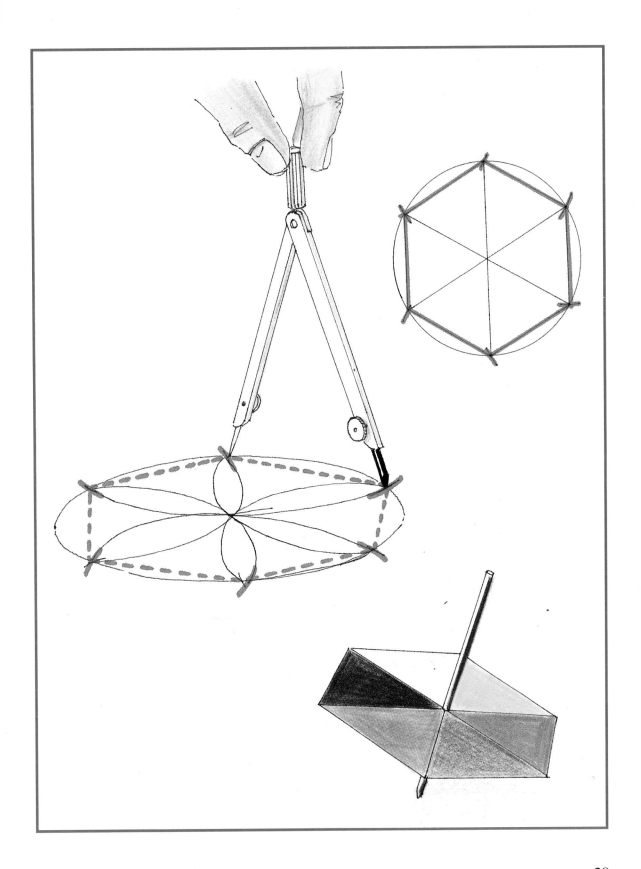

Tic-tac-toe, which is also known as Noughts and Crosses, is a very well-known and easy game for two players. Draw a double cross made of two horizontal and two vertical lines on a square piece of cardboard. One player draws "O" (Noughts) and the other "X" (Crosses), taking turns to draw one at a time in one of the nine spaces. The aim of the game is to get three of the same signs in a line, horizontally, vertically, or diagonally.

To make the game more challenging, draw three crosses and play in three dimensions by imagining the three crosses one on top of the other. You can also increase the grid to four squares by four and try to get a line of four of your sign.

Another variation is to play with numbers. Draw a double cross. One player takes odd numbers from 1 to 9 inclusive, and the other has even numbers from 2 to 8 inclusive. The "odd" player goes first. Use each number only once. The challenge is to be the first to make a line of numbers which total 15.

Derrah, which is a game from Nigeria, is like Tic-Tac-Toe in its aim to make a row of three. It is also a game for two players. The grid is made up of six rows of seven columns, and each player needs twelve counters of his color.

Begin the game by placing all the counters on the board, taking turns. Any squares can be used. Then, each player in turn moves one counter at a time up, down, or sideways, but not diagonally, to try to make a row of three. Each time he does so, he takes one of his opponent's counters off the board. The game ends when one player cannot make any more rows of three; he is the loser.

One example of the many games based on noughts and crosses.

To play **Hangman**, you just need a pencil and paper. Any number can play. One player, who is the hangman, thinks of a word and places a row of dashes on the paper, with each dash standing for one letter of the word.

The other players take turns to guess a letter. If the letter appears in the word, the hangman must write it in its correct place on the dashes. If the letter appears more than once, the hangman must put it in for each appropriate dash.

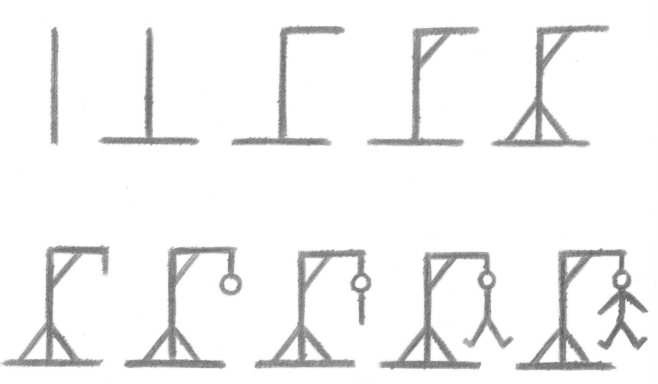

If the letter does not appear, the hangman starts to draw a gibbet, a noose, and a man hanging. Each time a wrong letter is called, the hangman adds a bit more to the drawing (see diagrams). If he completes the drawing before the other players guess the word, he has won and has another turn. If the others guess the word, the player who guessed it becomes the new hangman.

You can choose names of famous people, book titles, or animals, or any other category which interests you if you wish.

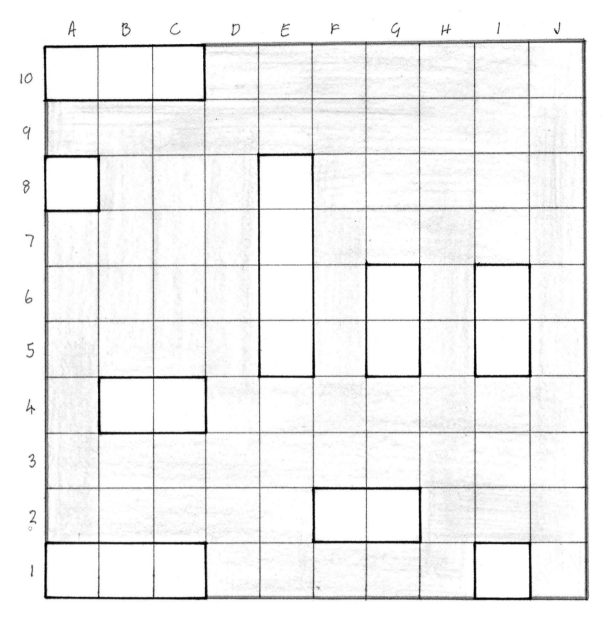

Graph paper is best if you want to play **Battleships**, which is a pencil and paper game for two players. Each player marks two identical grids of one hundred squares, numbered and lettered as shown. Then, without letting the other player see, each player marks on his grid the positions of 1 battleship (4 squares), 2 cruisers (3 squares each), 4 destroyers (2 squares each) and 2 submarines (1 square each). The ships must not touch each other at any point.

The players then take turns to name a square on the opponent's grid; for example, "B5." If that square contains part of

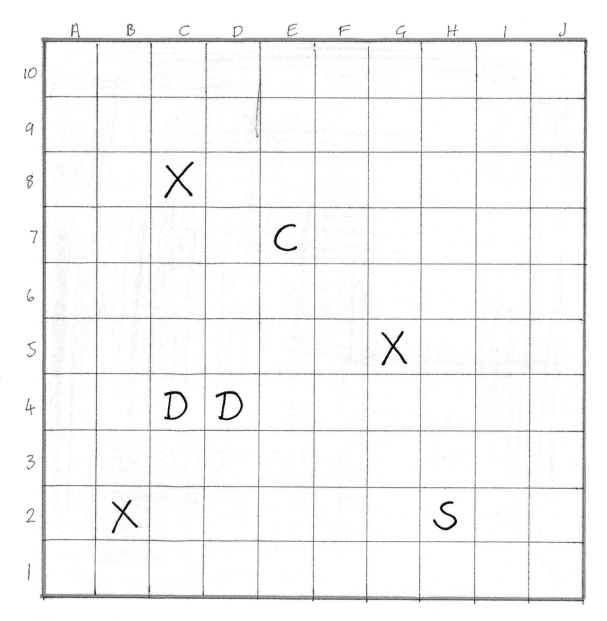

a ship or a submarine, the player must be truthful and say what kind of ship has been hit. If it was a submarine, he must, say that the submarine is sunk.

The object of the game is to sink all of your opponent's ships before he sinks yours. Keep a record of your shots on the second grid you drew at the beginning. If you remember how many squares each kind of ship is, and that no ship may touch another, it helps you to work out where the ships must be.

Boxes is another game for two which uses squares. Make a grid of dots on plain paper and take turns joining two dots

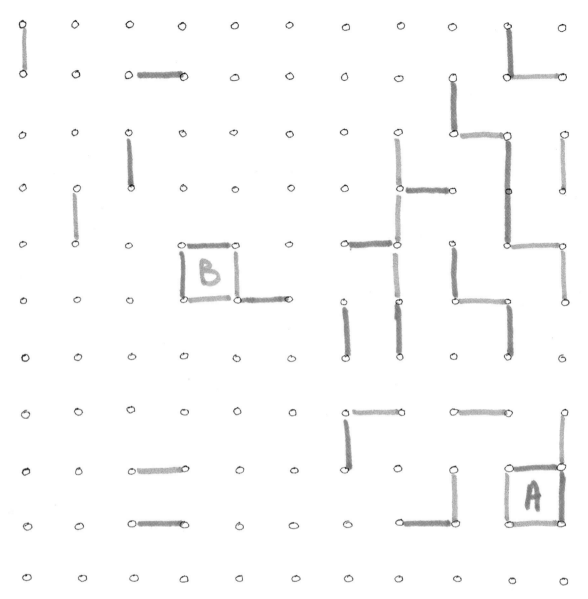

which are next to each other horizontally or vertically.

The aim is to be the player who draws the fourth line of a box to complete it. Label that box with your name or initial and have another turn. The player with the most boxes when the grid is complete is the winner.

To play **Sprouts**, you need two players and a piece of plain paper. Draw five dots on it at random. Each player takes turns to draw a line from one dot to another. The line does not have to be straight: it can be as long and twisted as you like. Then the player marks a new point anywhere she wishes on the line she has just drawn.

Above: **A game of Boxes in progress.**

Right: **A game of Sprouts.**

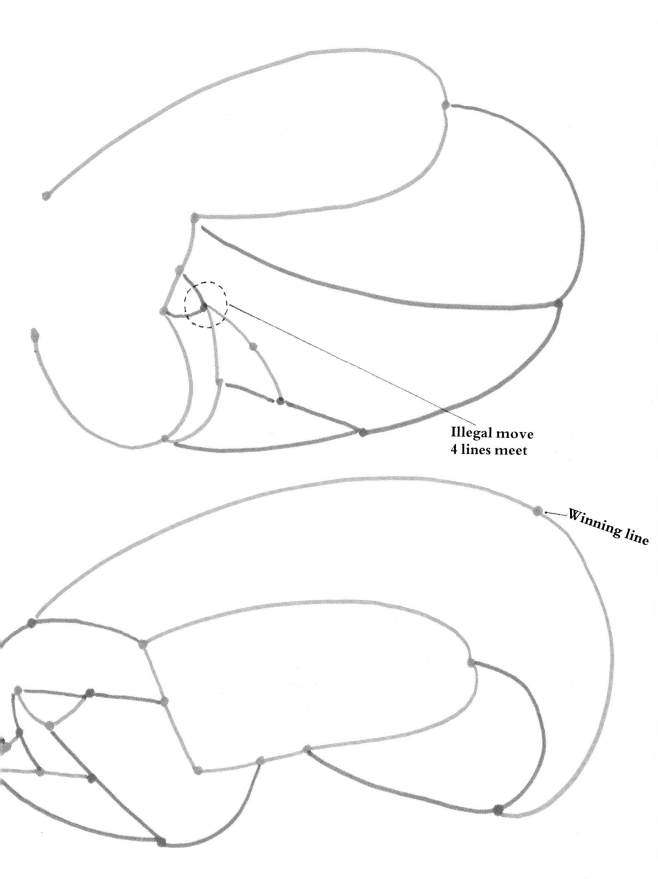

Illegal move
4 lines meet

Winning line

The other player then draws a line between any two points, including the one on the drawn line or not, as she chooses. But no line must cross another line, and no point may have more than three lines passing through it.

The winner is the player who draws the last line.

Goose Game is an old game from France. Draw a spiral on a large piece of paper or cardboard and divide it into forty-nine squares. Number them from the outside and work into the center. Label all the squares whose numbers can be divided by seven as "Goose." Label squares 10, 17, 25, and 30 "Inn;" squares 4, 23, 32, and 46 label "Toll Gate;" squares 5, 12, 19, and 40 "Bridges;" and squares 15 and 39 "Cricket."

Each player needs a counter, and you need a die or a spinner (see page 28). Take turns to throw and move according to the number shown. When you land on a "Goose" square, fly

A Nineteenth Century game of Goose.

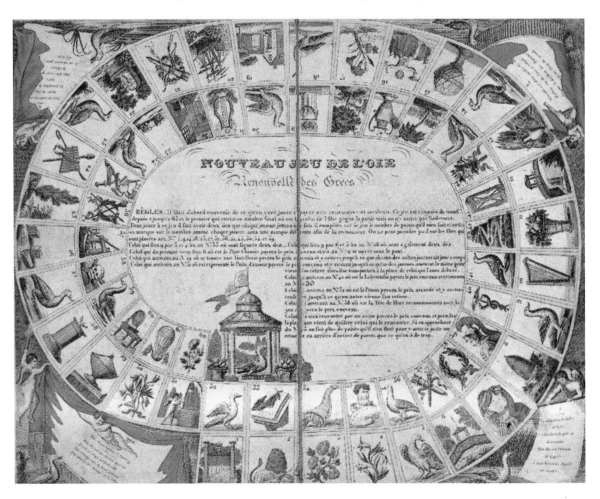

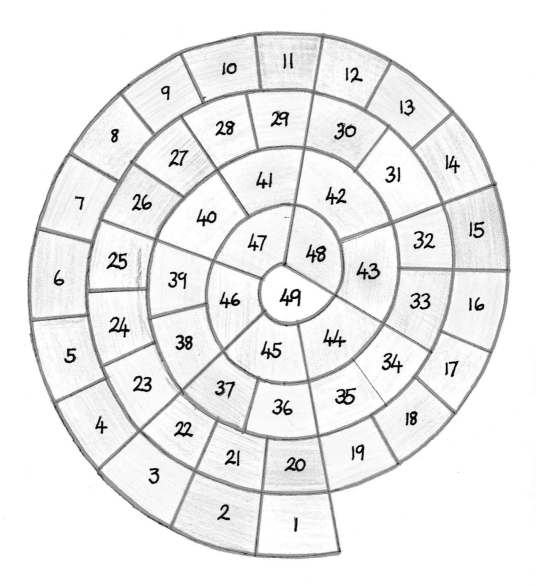

over the next two squares; if that would make you land on a penalty square, fly over that one as well. A "Bridge" square allows you to walk over the bridge to the next square.

The other labeled squares are all penalty squares. On an "Inn" square, you must wait there and miss a turn. At a "Toll Gate," you must go back one square. A "Cricket" square makes you go right back to square 1.

The winner is the first player to get to square 49 and fly out of the Goose Garden.

During the French Revolution, the labeled squares were changed so that they were topical. You could adapt the game, too — perhaps it could have a Space theme.

Snakes and Ladders may be related to the Goose Game, although it probably also has connections with a Hindu religious game in which the snakes represented vices and the ladders virtues.

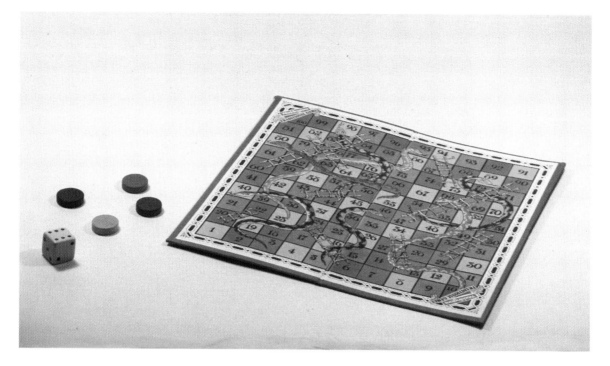

Troy Town is another very old maze game. It has been brought up to date as a computer game, but is also fun to play with pencil and paper. Basically, one player draws a maze for the other players to try to get through. The maze designer can adjust the difficulty of the maze according to the ages of the players, but he must make sure he can do it himself! Ask people to start either from the middle and try to get out, or start from the entrance and try to get to the middle.

There was a famous ancient maze, or labyrinth, on the Greek island of Crete where the Minotaur, a creature which was half-bull and half-man, was supposed to live. He devoured humans who were punished by being put in the maze. Stone mazes have been found all over northern Europe and Scandinavia. At Hampton Court Palace in England, there is a famous maze made of hedges which is nearly 500 years old.

Consequences is a party game for all ages and any number of people. All each person needs is a pencil and a piece of paper

A modern Snakes and Ladders board; you can design and make your own game very easily.

40

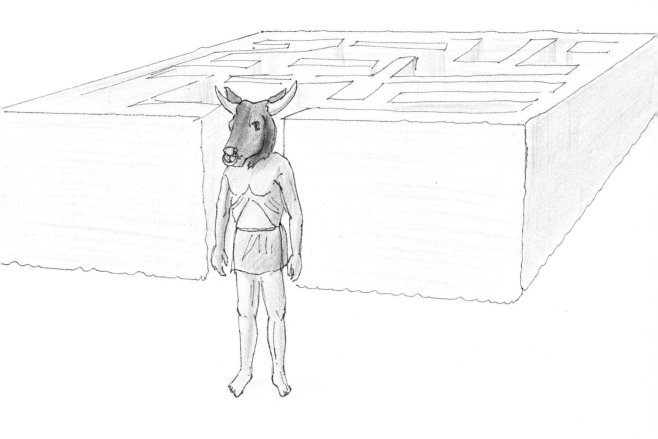

Minotaur guards his maze in the game of Troy Town.

about 4 inches wide and about 10 inches long. The players sit forming a circle. At the top of the paper each person writes a female name: it can be just any girl's name or it can be the name of a famous person or character from a book, film or television series. Without revealing what is written on the paper each person folds over the top so that the name is covered and passes it to the person on her right.

Next, everybody writes a masculine name just beneath where the paper is folded over. The paper is folded over again and passed to the right. This procedure is repeated to write what she said, what he said and what was the consequence. The consequence means the result or what happened.

To finish the game each person opens out the paper she has just received and tells the story on her paper. For example: "Shirley Temple met Pluto at the White House. She said, 'What's up, Doc?' He replied, 'Have you seen Roger Rabbit?' and the consequence was twelve piglets." Obviously the more imaginative you are, the funnier the stories will be.

SHIRLEY TEMPLE

PLUTO

AT THE WHITE HOUSE

Whats up doc?

Have you seen
Roger Rabbit?

12 Piglets

You can use the same idea to draw crazy figures in **Picture Consequences.** The first player draws the head. The second draws the body from the neck to the waist. The third fills in the body from the waist to the ankles and the last player draws the feet. You have to be careful to make the folds so that the drawing joins up.

At Christmas it is fun to make stars for decorations and there is a very easy way to make them out of paper just by folding and cutting. Take a piece of paper about 8 inches by 10 inches and fold it in half vertically. Keeping it folded fold again, this time horizontally. Lay the paper so that the corner with the double fold is at the bottom right and fold the bottom left corner over to the right hand edge. Then fold over the sloping edge again to meet the right hand edge. Finally make slanting

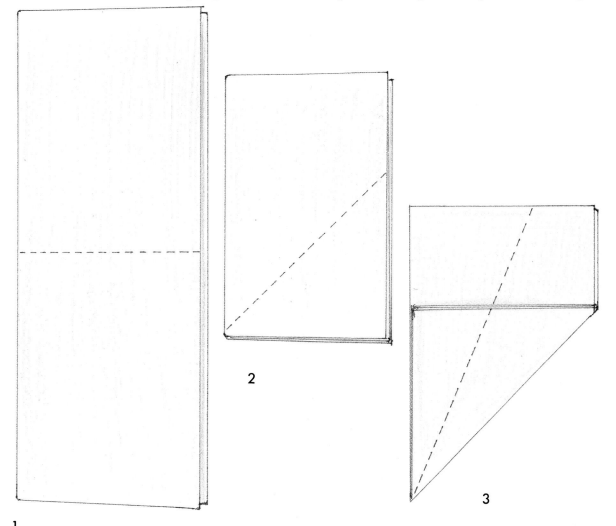

1

2

3

cuts as shown in the diagrams. When you unfold your paper, you will have a perfect eight-pointed star if you have folded accurately. Once you have got the idea, you can experiment to vary the shape and number of points on your stars. Also try using different colored papers and sticking pairs of stars together.

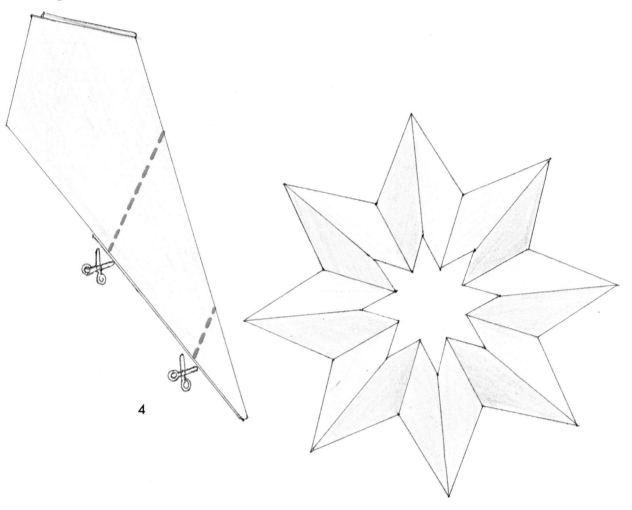

4

If you are interested in making some of the suggestions in this book it is a good idea to save used pieces of paper, such as old computer print-out sheets, so that you can use them for practice. You can buy sheets of colored construction paper for your final efforts. This book is a starting point; if you want to know more, look for books about origami, paper sculpture, and mathematical models.

Glossary

at random   Not in any special order.

bridle   Part of a kite which allows the body of the kite to fly at a right angle so that it catches the breeze.

diagonal   A line or fold from one corner to the opposite corner.

circumference   The distance around the edge of a circle.

devout   Following the demands of one's religion dutifully.

gibbet   An upright post with an arm on which the bodies of criminals who had been executed were hung as a warning to others.

Hindu   Having to do with the Indian religion of Hinduism which worships several gods.

horizontally   In a straight line from left to right.

intersect   The point at which two or more lines meet or cross each other.

Oriental   From countries east of the Mediterranean Sea, especially those of Eastern Asia.

parallelogram   A closed shape made from two pairs of parallel lines.

parallel lines   Always remain the same distance apart; they never met.

radius   Any line drawn from the center of a circle to a point on its circumference.

rectangle   A parallelogram which has four right angles. (oblong)

right angle   An angle between two lines which measures 90 degrees; a quarter turn.

square   A closed shape made of four equal straight lines in which each corner is a right angle.

taut   Held tight and straight.

toll gate   A barrier which no one is not allowed to pass until they have paid a fee.

topical   Having to do with events that have recently happened.

triangle   A closed shape made of three straight lines.

vertically   In a straight line up and down.

vices   Faults of character, bad habits.

Index of Countries

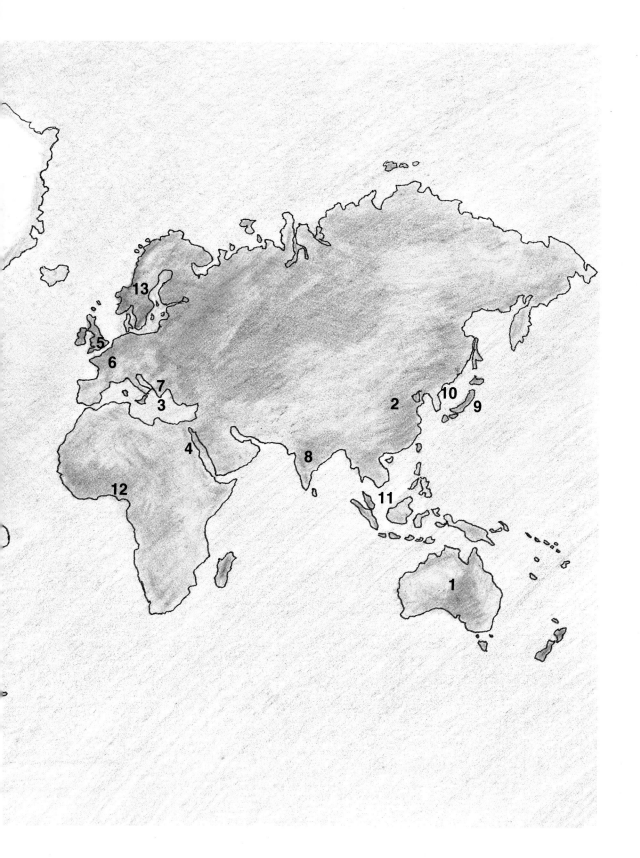

Index